Aisha **Ben** **Cassie** **Don** **Emily**

Have a good time at the local Fun Fair with your friends, but when you visit the Hall of Mirrors you will all find yourselves trapped inside a

HAUNTED MAZE!

Frank **Gloria** **Harry** **Iris** **Theo**

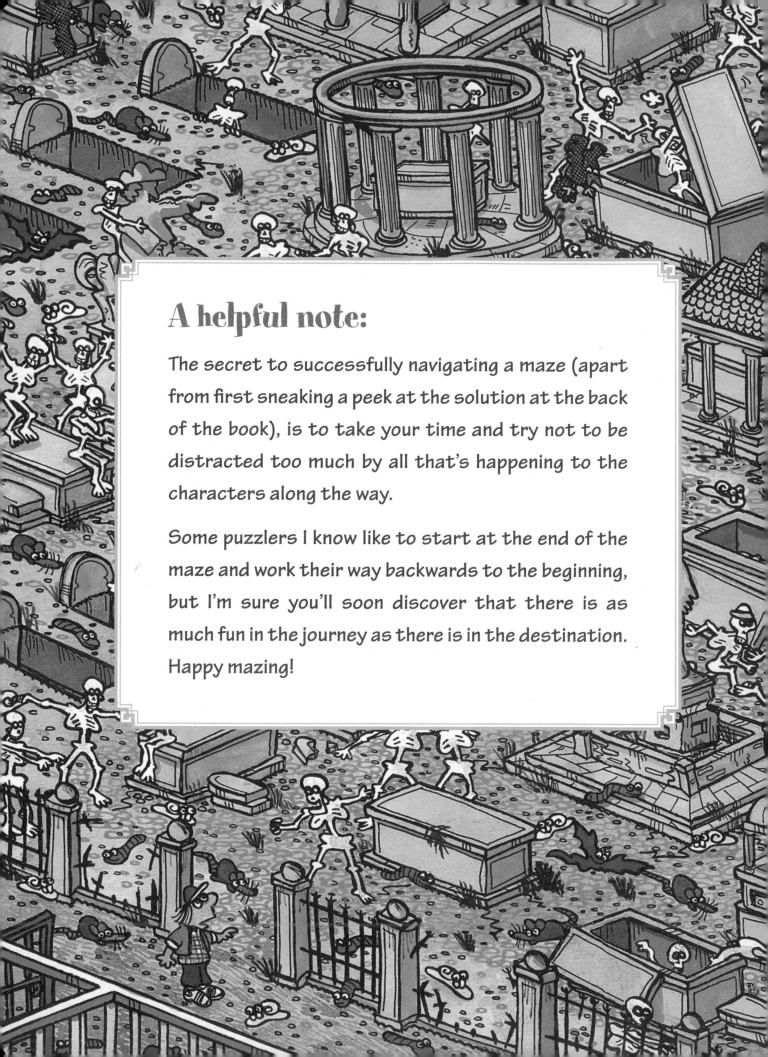

A helpful note:

The secret to successfully navigating a maze (apart from first sneaking a peek at the solution at the back of the book), is to take your time and try not to be distracted too much by all that's happening to the characters along the way.

Some puzzlers I know like to start at the end of the maze and work their way backwards to the beginning, but I'm sure you'll soon discover that there is as much fun in the journey as there is in the destination. Happy mazing!

Here are some questions to answer along the way:

1. In which maze do you see a bat sleeping?

2. Which letter of the alphabet can't you see on any of the blocks in "The Rescue"?

3. Where does Emily find herself sitting next to a ghost?

4. Who finds the map that helps you all to escape and where?

5. How many monsters do you have to creep past in order to complete the "Sleeping Monsters" maze?

6. Where does Iris pick up a worm?

7. Where can you see a one-legged soldier?

8. Where does Theo get a hug?

9. In which maze can you see sharks?

10. Where, apart from in "Skeletons Galore," can you see a skeleton?

11. Where does Gloria get picked up by a bat?

12. Which is the only maze before "The Rescue" where one of the children doesn't go missing?

13. One new type of animal appears in each maze and then appears in every maze from then on. In which maze do each of the animals to the right first appear?

* Solutions for this page can be found on page 29.

THE HALL OF MIRRORS

The new Hall of Mirrors attraction at the local Fun Fair looks exciting. But once inside you and your friends find that it is impossible to reach the exit. The only way out is an opening to the left of the exit sign, which will lead you to a series of spooky and dangerous mazes.

EXIT

5

THE BLACK PATH

Now you have to follow the Black Path to some stone steps leading downward at the center of the pit. Whatever you do, don't step off the path.

THE ACID CAVE

At the bottom of the steps you find yourself in a cave. The way out is through the tunnel, but to get to it you must carefully avoid the pools of blue acid.

SLEEPING MONSTERS

What's this! Monsters in cages! But you can pass them safely if you are very quiet and if you always move into an empty cage after creeping through a cage with a monster in it.

10

11

SKELETONS GALORE

After safely getting past the monsters you must now make a dash for the big house, and to reach it you will have to avoid the skeletons. If you run quickly you can get there before the skeletons have time to move.

THE GIANT SPIDER

Inside the house you find a series of rickety wooden paths. The Giant Spider will only be alerted if any of you step onto one of the creaky, red, loose floorboards on your way through the maze.

GHOST TRAIN
Now it's into the carriages of the Ghost Train. Ride the rails and try to reach the far end without ending up back where you started. Have you noticed by now that most of your friends are missing?

THE KEY

Frank has a map which might get you out of the Haunted Maze. First you will need to get the key from the table in the main hall. To avoid the scorpions you'll need to start at Emily's position and swing from chandelier to chandelier until you reach the big one in the center where you can drop to the table below. You can't use the chandeliers hanging in pairs as your weight will unbalance them, so only use the ones hanging singly.

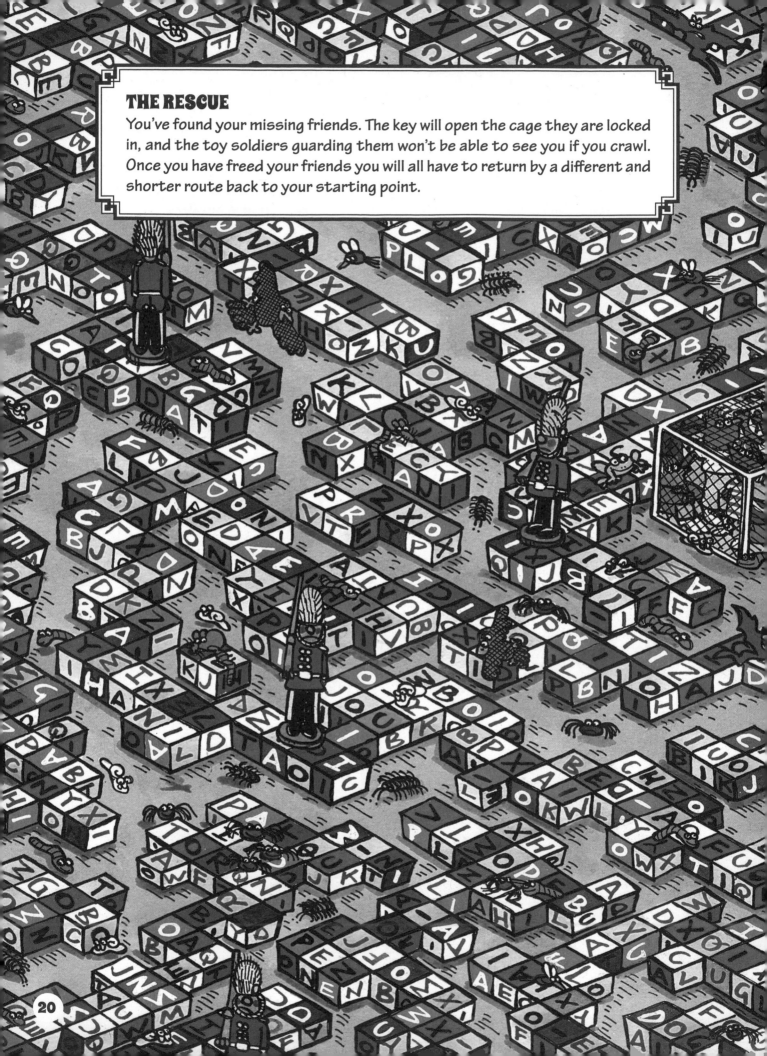

THE RESCUE

You've found your missing friends. The key will open the cage they are locked in, and the toy soldiers guarding them won't be able to see you if you crawl. Once you have freed your friends you will all have to return by a different and shorter route back to your starting point.

HEADLESS GHOSTS
The map has shown you an escape route through the grand-father clock at midnight. The Headless Ghosts are blocking your way but you can confuse them if you all split up into pairs and take five different routes back to the Fun Fair.

SOLUTIONS

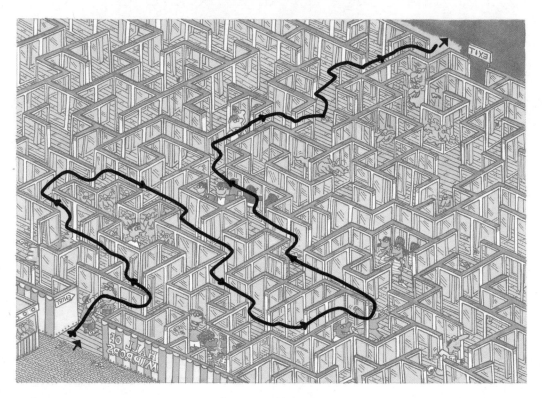

The Hall of Mirrors
pages 4-5

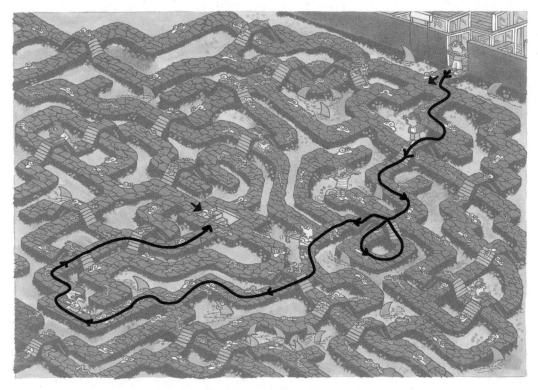

The Black Path
pages 6-7

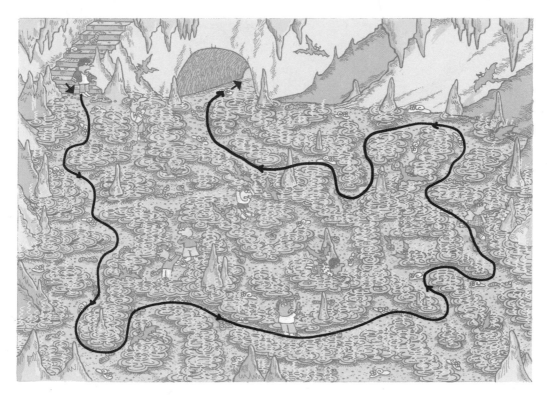

The Acid Cave
pages 8-9

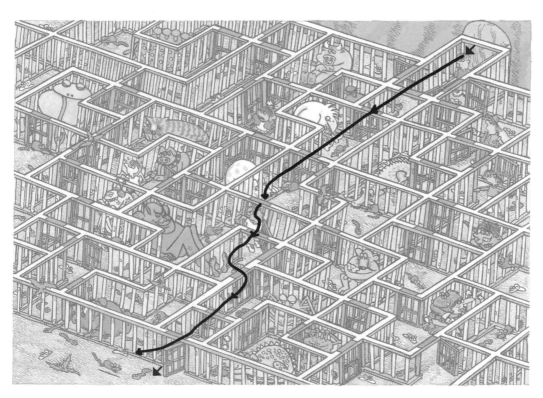

Sleeping Monsters
pages 10-11

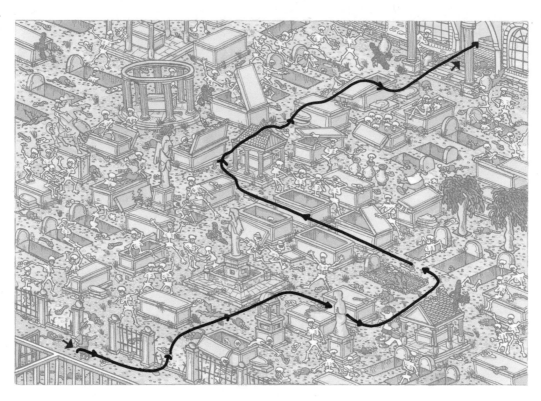

Skeletons Galore
pages 12-13

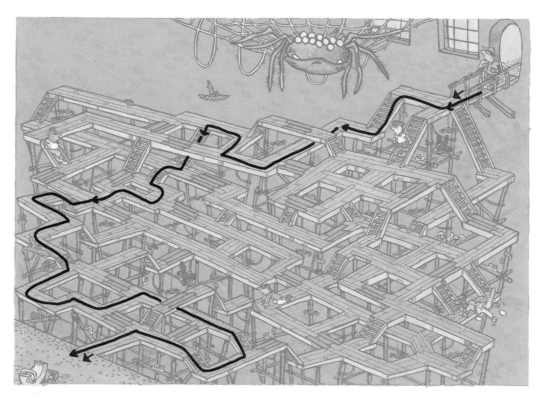

The Giant Spider
pages 14-15

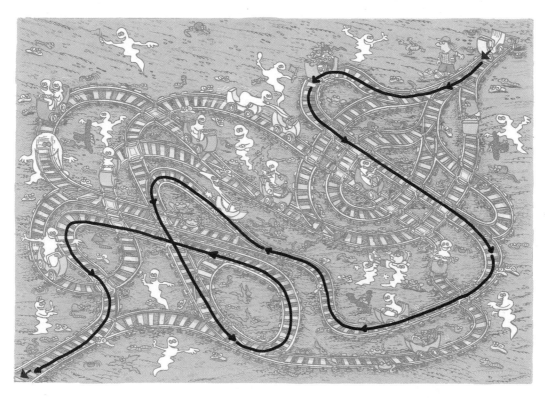

Ghost Train
pages 16-17

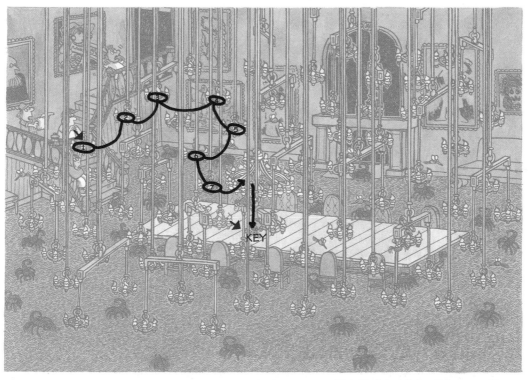

KEY

The Key
pages 18-19

Hint: The "single" chandeliers are all
colored blue — the "doubles" are all pink.

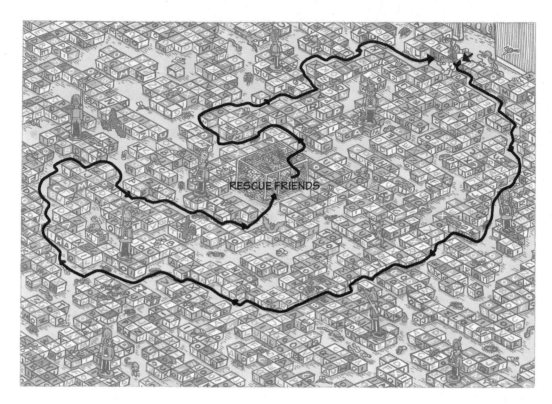

The Rescue
pages 20-21

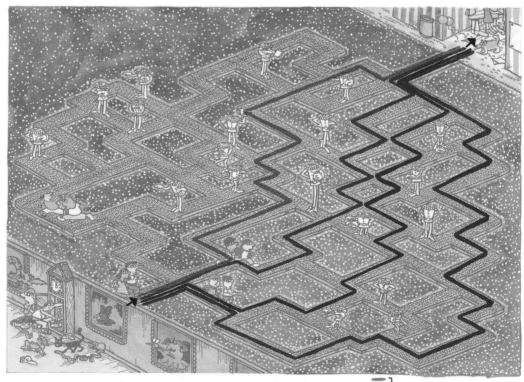

Headless Ghosts
pages 22-23

Solutions for the Maze Questions:

1. The Key

2. S

3. The Ghost Train

4. Frank in The Acid Cave

5. Three

6. The Black Path

7. The Rescue

8. Sleeping Monsters

9. The Black Path

10. The Giant Spider

11. The Acid Cave

12. The Ghost Train. Iris is picked up by ghosts but obviously is able to escape

13. Snails in The Hall of Mirrors
    Worms in The Black Path
    Red Bats in The Acid Cave
    Rats in Sleeping Monsters
    Ravens in Skeletons Galore
    Spiders in The Giant Spider
    Frogs in Ghost Train
    Mosquitoes in The Key
    Centipedes in The Rescue, and
    A Black Cat in Headless Ghosts

About the Author

I was born at quite an early age in the quaint English village of Liverpool. At school I was always drawing and started to send cartoons off to newspapers when I was ten years old. I got lots of nice letters in reply; however nobody published my drawings.

When I was sixteen my family moved to Whyalla in South Australia where I have lived ever since.

I spent my teenage years drawing comics and cartoons for fun, while still finding time to single-handedly animate a full-length movie on Super-8 film about the search for the Elephant's Graveyard.

When I was twenty-one I started to draw a regular cartoon called "The Stan Cartoon" for my local newspaper, which is still running today. A few years later I had my first strip cartoon published nationally. This was "Lafferty," set in the convict days of colonial Australia, and which ran for about twenty years and over six thousand strips.

I also self-published a number of comic books and illustrated quite a few books for various authors. Then one day I decided to try children's puzzle books and over the next ten years had over a dozen books published, including *The Hidden Puzzle Challenge* book for Dover Publications.

More recently I've published a series of *How To Draw* books, including *How to Draw Fantasy Figures, How to Draw Hands, How to Draw Circus Figures, How to Draw Aliens* and *Robots, How to Draw Australian Historical Figures*, and *How to Draw Pirates*. These grew out of a series of sheets I would hand out to students whenever I attended a school or library to conduct a cartoon-drawing workshop.

In all I think – it's hard to keep track – I've had over sixty books published.

When I'm not drawing I like to go out into my garage and play with my model soldier collection.

STEPHEN STANLEY..